Written by Dorine Barbey
Illustrated by Jean-Marie Poissenot

Specialist adviser:
Simon Pryce, B.Sc., F. Arbor. A.,
Arboricultural Association

THE WORKS

59p

ISBN 1 85103 147 2
First published 1992 in the United Kingdom
by Moonlight Publishing Ltd,
36 Stratford Road, London W8
Translated by Penny Stanley-Baker

POCKET • WORLDS

Woodland and Forest

Once upon a time,
forests were the home
of fairy tales…

If you go down to the woods today...

The tall trees towering above you cut out the light. It's so quiet, your own footsteps sound quite loud and a bit spooky. In fairy tales, woods are dark, mysterious places, where wolves, ogres and elves live. The deeper in you go, the more likely you are to get lost.

Long ago most of Britain was covered by a huge forest called the wildwood. In the forest lords hunted; in the forest, too, robbers hid.

The forest was cut down over the years, to make room for farms and villages.

The very first forests on Earth probably looked like this.

In a temperate climate like ours you find woodland of oak, beech and chestnut. These trees lose their leaves in the autumn

Mediterranean countries are hot and dry. The trees have small, leathery leaves. They keep their leaves in winter.

Conifers grow best in cold climates. The taiga forest where this thrush lives is a huge conifer forest in Siberia.

In the tropical forests tall trees tower over a dense jungle, home to all sorts of animals.

9

Each type of forest is a world of its own.

There is a great variety of trees and woodlands, depending on the climate, the altitude and the soil in which they grow. It is only where it is too dry or too cold that no trees will grow at all.
In California you find forests of giant sequoias or redwoods, the biggest trees in the world. In the mountains of China there are forests of bamboo, a sort of giant grass which pandas feed on.
In Australia koalas live high up in tall eucalyptus trees in the forest.

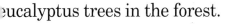

From little acorns
mighty oak trees grow.

In a good year a single oak tree
produces thousands of acorns.
Each acorn can become
a tree. If an acorn lands
on soft earth it produces
a small root and a shoot.

Each shoot grows into a baby oak tree
but it takes many years for the seedlings
to become a forest.
In fact only a handful of them will ever
grow into tall trees.

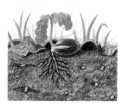

There is not enough space, light or water
for them all to survive. The weaker ones die.
The forester cuts down the fully grown
oak trees, once they are over a hundred
years old, to make way for the young oak.
The wood from the mature trees is sold
as timber oak. It is very strong and is good
for building.

At three years old, the seedlings are about a foot high. They have buds, bark and a spindly trunk.

By the time they are ten years old the oak trees are between 3 and 10 feet tall. They grow closely together in a thicket.

These tall, slim oaks are fifty years old.

Oaks are fully grown or mature at 100 to 200 years old.

14

In natural woodland, young trees grow up and take their chance as older ones die or fall down. Trees in a man-made forest, or plantation, need man's help to grow well. When mature trees are cut down, sprouts may grow from their stumps to form coppice, which can be cut for fencing sticks. Some woods have been managed by man for centuries, with woodmen looking after the trees carefully and cutting them at the right time.

The thick undergrowth of the coppice supports many plants and animals.

Hidden treasure on the forest floor.

Growing in the thick carpet of dead leaves
and twigs will be moss, fungi, bluebells,
cuckoo pint and lily of the valley.
Small insects, spiders, red ants
and centipedes live on the surface
in the leaf litter.
Under this top layer the leaves are being
eaten away by bacteria and fungi. They rot
down into a soft, fertile, crumbly earth
called humus.

**The woodland feeds and shelters
all kinds of animals.**
Earthworms burrow in and out aerating
the soil. Pheasants strut through
the undergrowth scratching for insects.
A rustle in the leaves may be a field vole
scuttling for cover.
Watch out for well-trodden badger paths.
In continental Europe, you may come across
families of wild boar or a striped fire
salamander asleep under a stone.
Bushy-tailed dormice curl up in nooks
and crannies, waiting for dark.

obins and nightingales build nests from
ead leaves, low in the tangled undergrowth.

n the shade,
nder the tall
ees, grow shrubs
nd climbing plants.
his is the undergrowth.
t is often prickly. Hawthorn
as bright red berries in autumn.
loe bushes bear purple berries the colour
f plums. Both are favourite foods for birds.

ear clearings and on the edge of the wood
he undergrowth is much thicker because
lore light gets through to the plants.
racken and brambles bar the way.

he bushes in the undergrowth come
to leaf early, before the foliage of the tall
ees overhead cuts out their light.

urtle doves nest
hawthorn bushes.
◄ In the foreground
a swallowtail butterfly;
rare visitor.

he dormouse often builds
s round ball of a nest in the fork
a tree well above the ground.

On a walk in the woods you might spot a nuthatch, a squirrel, a greater spotted woodpecker, a roe deer and a fox, but not a lynx. They live in the forests of North America and continental Europe.

s day breaks the woods come alive.

o down to the woods early and find
good hiding place. If you keep still,
ou may hear a woodpecker drilling away
t the bark of a tree, or see a nuthatch
campering down a tree trunk head first.
hey are looking for insects to eat.
here could be a fox skulking
ı the undergrowth, waiting
or a bird or a rabbit.
ine martens sometimes
unt squirrels. Deer nibble
t young shoots. Insects,
ıeat-eaters (carnivores)
nd plant-eaters (herbivores)
ll have their place
ı the forest
od chain.

he hoopoe, another insect-eater

On the prowl: a stag beetle, antlers raised, a pine marten preparing to pounce, an eagle owl, a wild boar, a stag, two does, a fox chasing a hare and a foraging badger.

At night the wood can seem dark and frightening.

But not to the animals which come out of hiding then! Hares venture out into clearings. Badgers leave their setts and follow familiar paths in search of juicy worms and insects to eat. Before the rutting, or mating, season the stag marks out his territory and wards off intruders. Wild boar go rooting among the leaves for insects, snuffling and grunting.

An owl hoots in the trees and seconds later swoops down on an unsuspecting little wood mouse, vole or shrew. Sleepy hedgehogs uncurl and totter off on their spindly legs in search of grubs and beetles to eat.

The woodhen builds her nest in the ground. She is well camouflaged amongst the leaves.

The energy in the sun's rays causes leaves to release oxygen into the air which you breathe. In turn, plants need the carbon dioxide animals breathe out.

The forest is working day and night.

As they are warmed by the sun, leaves sweat small droplets of water which turn into clouds. From these clouds rain falls. The rain waters the forest. Fresh water flows from the forest into springs and streams. Plants and animals need each other to survive. They are part of a complicated woodland family in which each member plays an important part. The climate, soil type and terrain make up a delicate balance called an ecosystem.

The forest protects the soil. Roots bind it and prevent it being washed or blown away. Rotting leaves keep it fertile.

There are so many good things in the forest!

Fill your pockets with nuts and conkers. Watch out for wild strawberries and edible mushrooms. But never pick unknown berries or toadstools! Some are poisonous!

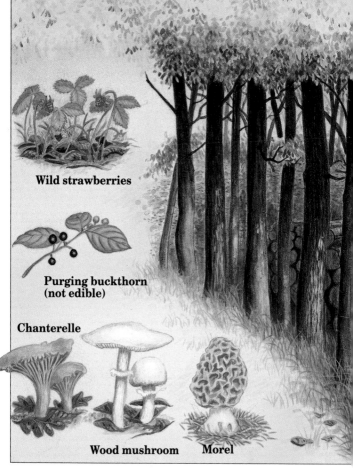

Wild strawberries

Purging buckthorn (not edible)

Chanterelle

Wood mushroom

Morel

And so many things that come from wood...

Wood harvested from forests is used for building and for making floorboards, furniture and fencing stakes. We burn wood and charcoal on our fires and wood pulp is used to make paper.

Charcoal burning is one of the oldest woodland crafts. The tightly-packed pieces of wood burn slowly into charcoal.

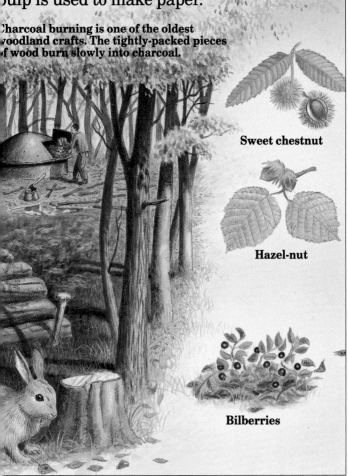

Sweet chestnut

Hazel-nut

Bilberries

Nowadays woodmen use chain-saws to fell the trees and strip them of their branches.

Young trees are planted in rows, evenly spaced, so that the forester can keep them free of weeds.

In some countries the sap, or resin, of pine trees is collected in a cup placed under a cut in the trunk.

The outer bark of the cork tree is peeled off every ten years, to make corks for bottles, floats for fishing lines and even buoys.

Woodmen fell the trees.
In the past they worked with axes.
The wood was dragged away on horse-drawn carts, or floated downstream.
Nowadays, once the felled trunks
are stripped of their branches, they are
picked up and stacked by powerful tractors
with cranes and loaded onto timber lorries
which take them to the sawmill.

Foresters look after the trees.
They plant new ones, clear away
weeds and dead branches,
thin out weaker trees and
check for pests and diseases.
They try to grow as many
good trees as they can.

In mountainous areas men used
to bring the sawn logs down
steep slopes on sledges.
Nowadays they use pulleys
and cables, or even
helicopters.

All over the world, trees and forests are at risk.

Around large towns, woods are felled
to make way for new roads
and buildings.

Pollution and acid rain harm trees and can
slow their growth. If trees die, plants
and animals that depend on them die too.

Fire is a great threat. Pine forests dry out
in summer. Fires spread quickly where
the undergrowth is not kept low.
Thousands of hectares of forest
go up in flames each year.

Where fire is a danger, broad strips
called fire-breaks are cleared of vegetation
to stop forest fires spreading.
There may be look-out towers as well.

Paper and cardboard are made from
fast-growing pine and spruce trees.
Timber for building and furniture
comes mostly from slower-growing trees
like oak, beech and ash.

Forest peoples

Yanomamo Indians live in the Amazonian rain forest, in wooden, leaf-thatched huts. Pygmies have lived in the heart of the African tropical forest for over 8000 years. They are small and wear clothes of tree bark. The men hunt animals using spears, arrows and nets. The women build the huts, weaving broad leaves in and out of a framework of bent poles. These peoples take no more from the forest than they need or than it can give. But modern ways of cutting these forests for timber and farming do not allow the trees to re-grow. Forests everywhere are disappearing.

The Akha tribe live in the hills of Thailand. They clear parts of the forest around their villages to grow rice and vegetables.

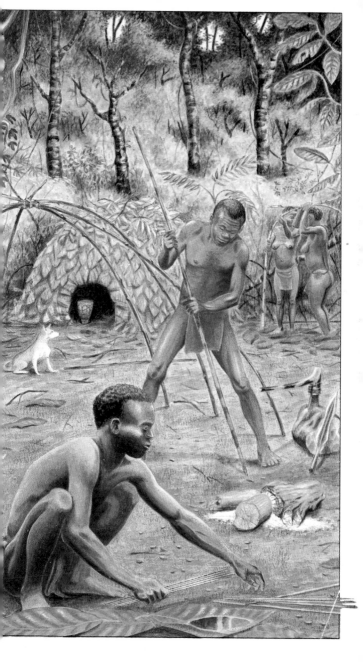

Build your own hut in the woods or in your garden. You will need some long straight sticks or bamboo canes and some string.

For the frame, choose two trees quite close together. Take a strong pole and tie it between the trees at about head height. Tie more poles together to make a frame and cover it with an old sheet.

Remember!

Get permission to build your shelter, and never cut living trees.

Don't leave litter behind you; it can endanger wildlife.

Index

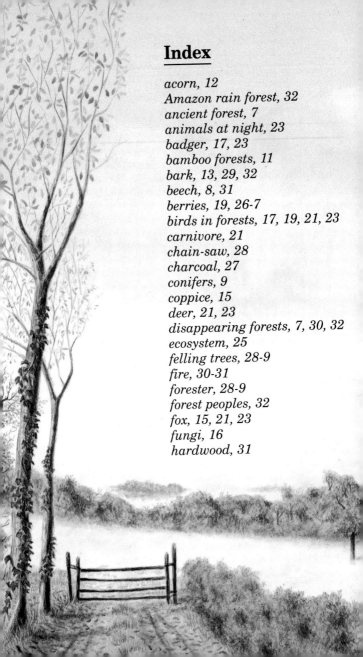

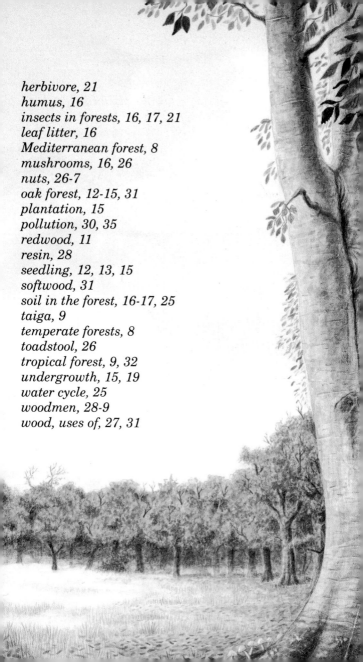

Pocket Worlds – building up into a child's first encyclopaedia: